Kevi

GW01158827

PONDERING WITH MARY

Fifteen Sonnets on the Mysteries of the Rosary

Illustrations by
Richard King

ST PAULS

ST PAULS Publishing
187 Battersea Bridge Road, London SW11 3AS

Copyright © ST PAULS UK 2000

ISBN 085439 579 2

Set by TuKan, High Wycombe
Produced in the EC
Printed by AGAM, Cuneo, Italy

ST PAULS is an activity of the priests and brothers
of the Society of St Paul who proclaim the Gospel
through the media of social communication

ACKNOWLEDGEMENTS

I wish to record my sincere thanks to Mr Kenneth King who on behalf of the King family gave me permission to reproduce in this book illustrations of the Mysteries of the Rosary, which were the work of his gifted father, Richard King.

Fr Benedict Cullen, OFM Cap., Archivist of the Capuchin Fathers, Church Street, Dublin, made these illustrations available, and I wish to thank him for his kindness, interest and invaluable advice on all occasions.

Photographic and reproduction work always require a high degree of technical expertise and attention to detail. These qualities were always present in the person of Catherine Lyons and were shared generously by her in the preparation of this book.

To my proof reader, Billy Gough, I offer a final and sincere word of thanks.

Kevin A. Laheen S.J.

INTRODUCTION

Throughout the centuries those who really loved Jesus, also loved Mary, his mother. In a special way poets, writers, artists and composers have used their art to honour her. It is in no way suggested that the following verses deserve a place among those masterpieces, nevertheless it is hoped that they may bring the reader closer to Mary, and deepen devotion to her. While this little book will be more at home in the prayer room or the bedroom rather than in the classroom or lecture hall, prayer groups will derive much help from it as they pray together.

Devotion to Mary finds its most popular expression in the Rosary. For centuries it has catered for the devotional needs of those who turn to her in prayer. While the traditional form is widely practised, other forms have been introduced to provide an element of variety, and for many have proved spiritually helpful. It is hoped that this book will introduce another method while preserving the essence of the Rosary, which is the contemplation of scriptural scenes in the context of devotion to Mary.

This book contains fifteen Sonnets on the Mysteries of the Rosary. There are also fifteen four-line verses on the same themes, and finally there are seven four-line verses on the Dolours, or Sorrows of Mary. On some occasions a preference to sing rather than recite the short verses has been expressed and accordingly a melody has also been provided for that purpose. The excellent illustrations by Richard King are intended to focus the attention on each Mystery as it is being contemplated.

These sonnets and verses can be used for individual recitation of the Rosary, but they are also intended for use in small groups. Young people have been enthusiastic about the shorter verses, and have also loved to sing rather than recite them. Some of them have found a mysterious delight in singing the final lines in Latin, rather than in the alternative English version provided.

HOW TO USE THIS BOOK

a. *For individuals*

The appropriate illustrations should be looked at very carefully.
Every detail ought to be noted and an effort made to discover the
message the artist wishes to convey. When the total picture is fixed
firmly in the mind, a very slow reading of the sonnet should
follow. The final two lines, which sum up the message, should be
dwelt on, and even repeated. A period of silent contemplation can
then follow, and the entire exercise concluded with one
Our Father, one Hail Mary and one Glory be to the Father. The
following Mysteries can then follow, using the same method.

b. *For groups*

A leader can explain briefly the essence of the Mystery to be
contemplated, which is then followed by a brief period of quiet
reflection on it. One Our Father, three Hail Marys and one Glory
be to the Father can then be recited, and the four-line verses
recited or sung according to the preference of the group, bringing
the exercise to a close. This method can then be repeated for the
following four Mysteries.

In translating the final Latin lines, slight liberties have been taken
occasionally in order that the metric and melodic accents may
coincide when the verses are sung. The use of the sonnets and the
short verses in no way deserve to be described as 'trimmings'.
They are part of the essence of the Mysteries which are being
contemplated, while the vocal recitation of the prayers, and the
singing of hymns, are intended to be conducive to that
contemplation.

As the title implies, this book provides matter to be *pondered*
rather than just *read* and put aside.

THE ANNUNCIATION, Luke 1:26-38

8

THE ANNUNCIATION

The gentle breath of March was in the air.
The rains had gone, the days grew long, the sun
Cast shorter shadows, and the trees once bare
Gave verdant proof that winter's work was done.

And somewhere on a hill above the town,
A new born lamb sent forth its infant bleat,
Op'ning its eyes on its first Spring. While down
Below upon a winding Nazareth street,

All unaware of lamb's or angel's voice,
The town folk passed their hours of toil and rest,
Unconscious of their reason to rejoice,
Since all in Mary's 'Fiat' had been blessed.

And while she worked her needle, thread and loom,
The Lamb of God took flesh in Mary's womb.

Reading: Luke 1:26-38

'Here I am, the servant of the Lord;
let it be with me according to your word.'

Lord Jesus,
open our hearts to the Holy Spirit
and make your home in us.

THE VISITATION OF MARY, Luke 1:39-42

THE VISITATION

Southward she made her way by vale and hill,
With early corn fields green to left and right.
Lost in her prayer and pondering until
Ain Karim's vineyards rose before her sight.

Two women to their Maker homage paid,
Gladd'ning each other in this visitation.
Two sons, One sinless and one sinless made
By power and presence of God's incarnation.

God looked on her and from her lowly state
Exalted her, and all will call her blessed
Through every age, and ever venerate
Her greatness, and pay honour to her, lest

It be forgotten how God favoured her,
His virgin Mother, his first Christopher.

Reading: Luke 1:39-56

'Blessed are you among women,
and blessed is the fruit of your womb!'

Lord Jesus,
give us the spirit of generosity
that we may serve you
unreservedly in others.

THE BIRTH OF JESUS, Luke 2:4-8

THE NATIVITY

The patient shepherds watched. The town folk slept.
The whole vast world seemed unaware that this
Clear night would see the fetters that had kept
Humanity in bondage break. The hiss

Of demons, then deprived of spoils, would ring
Through Hell, while silence balanced on a hill
Would reign till some angelic choir would sing
The birth of Christ in solitude. There, still

As yet unseen by shepherds' eyes, the Child
Lay in the straw. His Mother's faith aglow
She watched and prayed, while Joseph, husband mild,
Knelt too in adoration. Who could know

The meaning of this birth, to some so odd?
Yet here, through faith, we greet enfleshed our God.

Reading: Luke 2:1-21

*'She gave birth to her firstborn son
and wrapped him in bands of cloth,
and laid him in a manger.'*

*Lord Jesus,
be born again in me today,
and help me to see you in the world
and in all human beings.*

THE PRESENTATION OF JESUS, Luke 2:22-25

THE PRESENTATION

They came to make the off'ring their Child
To God, and then redeem Him as the law
Prescribed. They were unknown, and no one smiled
A welcome to this trio. Then they saw

A man approach them, tall and dignified.
He gazed, then took the Child and held Him fast,
'You may dismiss me now, O Lord,' he cried,
'The promised Saviour I have seen at last'.

And Mary then rejoiced that by this man
Her Son was known as the expected One;
The One all hoped for since the world began.
She took Him in her arms again, God's Son.

But Mary's joy in giving to the Lord,
Was tempered by the prophet's promised sword.

Reading: Luke 2:22-40

*'My eyes have seen your salvation
which you have prepared
in the presence of all peoples.'*

*Lord Jesus,
let me first be pruned
so that I may bear fruit
and witness to the salvation
you have brought to the world.*

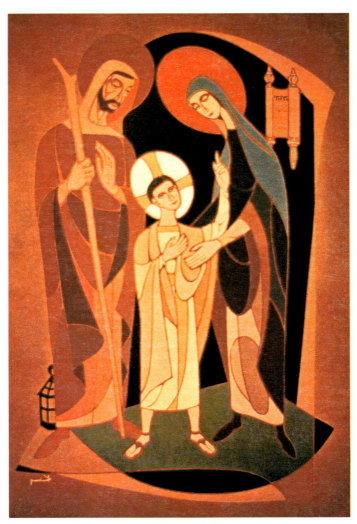

THE FINDING OF JESUS IN THE TEMPLE, Luke 2:46-49

THE FINDING OF JESUS IN THE TEMPLE

And twelve years later, once again she stood
Within the Temple, dulled and numbed by pain
And anguish for the loss of Jesus. Could
This be the sword, which time and time again

She had recalled that Simeon had said
Long years ago would one day pierce her heart?
Could He be stolen, kidnapped, even led
Away to be a captive in some part

Of Rome's great empire, never to be seen
By her again? Among some cruel men
He well might die, and joys that might have been
Would vanish. But she prayed, and searched, and then

She suddenly had reason to rejoice,
When through the Temple's din she heard His voice.

Reading: Luke 2:41-52

'Why were you searching for me?
Did you not know
that I must be in my Father's house?'

Lord Jesus,
grant me the grace
to imitate you in placing
your Father's kingdom first.

THE AGONY IN THE GARDEN, Luke 22:39-46

THE AGONY IN THE GARDEN

Day time has passed when I may safely walk.
The stumbling time of night has settled down.
Across the Kedron men now laugh and talk.
Tomorrow they will dress me like a clown.

O Peter, James, and John, where are you now?
Could you not watch a single hour with me?
Well may you sleep! Have you forgotten how
I told you once that man's iniquity

Would bring on me this anguish and this pain,
The scourging, mocking and the crowning sore
And death? O God, for many all in vain.
Frustration now bleeds free from every pore.

This cruel, bitter chalice, God, I shun.
Yet not my will but Thine alone be done.

Reading: Luke 22:39-46

'Father, if you are willing,
remove this cup from me;
yet, not my will but yours be done.'

Lord Jesus,
in all our trials and sufferings,
teach us to pray
that God's will may be done.

THE SCOURGING AT THE PILLAR, Mark 15:9-15

THE SCOURGING AT THE PILLAR

'I find no case in Him; He must go free.'
'If you release Him you're not Caesar's friend.'
Thus hatred born of man's iniquity
Would joust with weakness winning in the end.

And compromise and flattery and fear
Would all be used to set the Prisoner free.
But all these weapons powerless were. For here
They faced the men whose proud authority

Would see their Victim dead upon a cross
And nothing less. Then Pilate gave consent
To have Him scourged with savage blows and loss
Of blood, while priestly faces smiled assent.

Then Roman cowardice washed its hands of blame,
While Roman justice hung its head in shame.

Reading: Matthew 27:21-26

*'What should I do with Jesus who is called the
Messiah? Why, what evil has he done?'*

*Lord Jesus,
present in all those who suffer,
give me the strength to heal broken hearts.*

THE CROWNING WITH THORNS, Matthew 27:27-31

THE CROWNING WITH THORNS

Power and pride and strength are what we meet
In men who lord it over men as kings.
With armies massed they hunger to defeat
Their latest foe, and capture all the things

That form the spoils of deeds of daring done.
Not so our King. He claims no conquering sword,
Nor trophies that can point to battles won.
He does not kill, but life comes from His word.

For He is gentle, and concerned that all
Should live in peace, with rancour set apart,
He yearns that all should harken to His call
And share the treasures of His loving Heart.

He loves all sinners, sin alone He scorns,
Our King who for us wore the Crown of Thorns.

Reading: Matthew 27:27-31

*'They stripped him
and put a scarlet robe on him,
and after twisting some thorns into a crown,
they put it on his head.'*

*Lord Jesus,
help me to remove a thorn where I can
and to plant a flower in its place.*

THE CARRYING OF THE CROSS, John 19:16-19

2 4

THE CARRYING OF THE CROSS

My God, they've placed a cross upon my back.
I hear the shouts of triumph from my foes.
My head is bruised, my flesh is torn, for lack
Of sleep I falter, almost faint. And those

Who would destroy me do not realise
It is for love of them I start this trek,
Which ends in death before the very eyes
Of friend and foe. O Loving Father, check

This faintness. Strengthen me in every way
Along the road that leads to Calv'ry's hill.
Love drives me on, let no one ever say
I faltered or I failed to do Thy will.

With every step I take beneath this cross,
Let love abound and wipe away man's loss.

Reading: Luke 23:26-31

*'As they led him away,
they seized a man, Simon of Cyrene,
and laid the cross on him,
and made him carry it behind Jesus.'*

*Lord Jesus,
give me strength
to deny myself and take up my cross,
and follow you.*

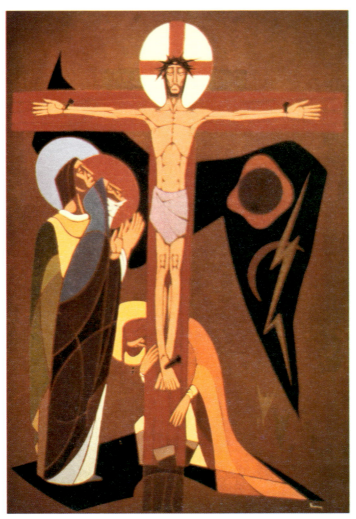

THE CRUCIFIXION AND DEATH OF JESUS, Luke 23:44-47

THE CRUCIFIXION

It was the day when night would come at noon;
When rocks would split and terror fill the air;
When Roman soldiers' mortal work would soon
Be done, and men would scoff and taunt. And there

Beneath the cross a vigil would be kept
By His devoted few, while some would stay
A distance off, ashamed because they slept
Throughout His agony. For on this day

To show beyond all doubt His love for men
Christ willingly and innocent would die.
Sharp thorns would pierce His sacred head, and then
A spear His heart, and thus in death He'd lie,

But we are now redeemed in God's pure sight,
Since Christ was sacrificed in noon-day night.

Reading: Luke 23:33-49

*'Father,
into your hands I commend my spirit.'*

*Lord Jesus,
teach me self-abandonment
to your Father's love.*

THE RESURRECTION, Matthew 28:5-8

THE RESURRECTION

Since Friday there had been a sense of doom
In all their hearts. Then suddenly they heard
The breathless voice of Magdalene, 'The tomb'
She said, 'is empty', and their sorrow shared

Gave place to action. Rumour, too, was rife.
The women said that angels had been seen
And doubt and dawning faith were locked in strife.
Then Magdalene recounted how she'd been

Addressed by Jesus. Later Peter, too,
Had met Him. And two travellers also said
He'd walked with them, and later that they knew
Him when He took, and blessed and broke the bread.

They prayed that all their lingering doubts would cease.
Then suddenly He came and whispered, 'Peace.'

Reading: Luke 24:1-12

*'Why do you look for the living among the dead?
He is not here; but has risen.'*

*Lord Jesus,
let me be reminded of your Resurrection
in every act of
forgiveness, trust, friendship,
and in our faith
which would otherwise be in vain.*

THE ASCENSION OF JESUS, Luke 24:50-53

THE ASCENSION

They called to mind the previous forty days
As they assembled with Him on the Mount
Of Olives; how in unexpected ways
He came and went – how often? – None could count.

And there He talked, instructions, too, He gave
That they should journey ceaselessly and preach
His message, and through baptism help to save
The world. Their ministrations were to reach

All nations. That His Kingdom, too, should last,
He said the promised Paraclete He'd send,
Assuring them, as ever in the past,
He would be with them till the world should end,

And in the splendour of that Thursday's light,
He blessed them, and ascended from their sight.

Reading: Mark 16:14-20

*'Go into all the world and proclaim the
good news to the whole creation.'*

*Lord Jesus,
help me to be a witness
to the good news of your kingdom.*

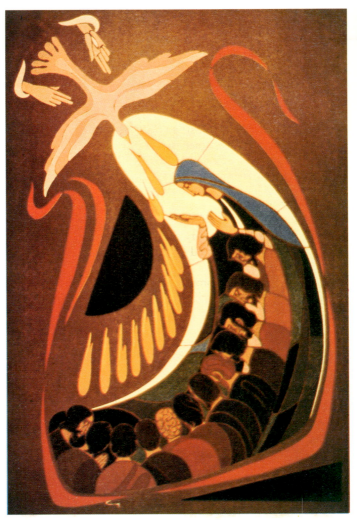

THE COMING OF THE HOLY SPIRIT, Acts 2:1-5

THE COMING OF THE HOLY SPIRIT

There was a sound as if a mighty wind
Had thundered through the city on its course.
And shafts of wisdom entered every mind
Of His elect, and by the very force

Of Pentecostal gifts, they lost all fear.
With courage they proclaimed the Risen Lord.
And stranger still, all foreigners could hear
That message in their native tongue. Each word

Was charged with fire born of the Paraclete,
And fortitude and knowledge never known
Were witnessed then on every city street,
While praising voices turned to Heaven's throne.

And thus the world was brought to life from death,
Sustained and quickened by the Spirit's breath.

Reading: John 14:15-26

*'The Holy Spirit,
whom the Father will send in my name,
will remind you of all that I have said to you.'*

*Come, O Holy Spirit,
and kindle in us
the fire of your love.*

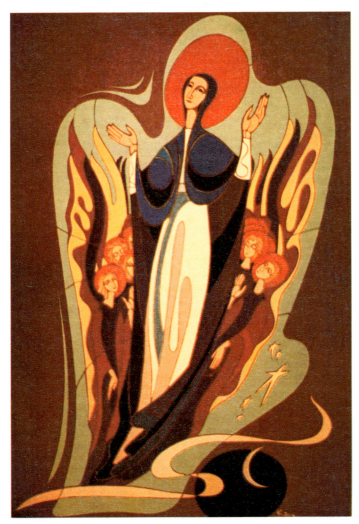

THE ASSUMPTION OF MARY

THE ASSUMPTION

'The Lord is with you' – many years ago
The voice of Gabriel was heard to say,
And Mary through her life would clearly show
How true it was. For from the very day

Her name was first inscribed on Scripture's page,
She stayed with Him; should she appear alone,
She searched for Him alike through every age
From infancy until He did atone

For all our sins upon the cross. And so
This outward symbol of her unity
Of heart and mind with Him must surely show
Her union with Him through eternity.

And when at length her earthly course had run,
God fittingly assumed her to her Son.

Reading: Revelation 12:1-17

'A great portent appeared in heaven:
a woman clothed with the sun,
with the moon under her feet,
and on her head a crown of twelve stars.'

Father, you did great things for the Virgin Mary,
and brought her, body and soul, to the glory of heaven.
Fill the hearts of your children with the hope of
Christ's glory.

THE CORONATION OF MARY, Revelation 11:19; 12:1-2

THE CORONATION

There is a sign of grandeur in a crown,
A queen will wear it in her subjects' name.
It symbolises power, and all bow down
To show respect, and manifest their claim

On her. And she in turn will always show
Her care for them, and her sincere concern
For all their needs. We have a Queen we know
Who'll care for us, and lovingly discern

Our smallest need. For she was crowned above
In Heaven's court that she might intercede
With Jesus for us, prompted by that love
That won from Him His first miraculous deed.

Thus all of us believe, yet none know how
She reigns, our Queen, in God's eternal now.

Reading: Luke 1:46-55

*'All generations will call me blessed;
for the Mighty One has done great things for me,
and holy is his name.'*

*Mary, my Mother,
pray for me that I may
one day share in your joy
and see the Father in all his glory.*

THE JOYFUL MYSTERIES

The Annunciation

The angel came on shrill March day,
God's message at Mary's feet to lay,
'Fiat', she said, and knelt to pray,
    Et Verbum caro factum est.
    And Christ assumed our human flesh

The Visitation

She left her house without delay.
By hill and vale she made her way,
And heard an ageing cousin say,
    Ave Beatissima.
    All hail to you, most blessed one

The Nativity

In late December, dark and cold,
While sheep were safe in kindly fold,
Then happened what had been foretold,
    Puer nobis natus est.
    Unto to us a Child is born

The Presentation

And in the Temple of the Lord,
A man held God's Eternal Word,
God's promised One, our rich reward,
    Nunc me dimittis, Domine.
    You may dismiss me now, O Lord

The Finding

And in the Temple once again
She sought her Son with anxious pain,
And found Him. May He long remain,
    Nobiscum semper Dominus.
    With us for ever as Our Lord

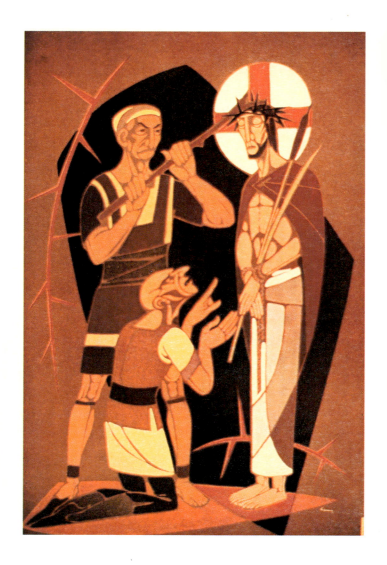

40

THE SORROWFUL MYSTERIES

The Agony

> At dead of night all secretly,
> His agony for you and me,
> Was suffered in Gethsemane.
> > Jesus Christus passus est.
> > *Jesus kneels in agony*

The Scourging

> They drew the lash with all their might,
> The blows fell fast from left and right,
> A tortured, bruised and bleeding sight.
> > Jesus flagellatus est.
> > *Christ is scourged by cruel men*

The Crowning

> A King in purple sat forlorn
> His flesh bespittled, rent and torn,
> And on His head a crown of thorn,
> > Jesus coronatus est.
> > *Christ, the Lord, is crowned with*
> > *thorns*

The Via Dolorosa

> He walked along that bitter road,
> He fell three times beneath His load,
> But on the way what love He showed.
> > Jesus oneratus est.
> > *Christ is burdened by His cross*

The Crucifixion

> Against the sky on Calv'ry's height,
> Three roods stand out. The Lord of light,
> Is crucified in noon-day night.
> > Jesus crucifixus est.
> > *Christ the Lord is crucified*

THE GLORIOUS MYSTERIES

The Resurrection

Upon the cross they saw Him dead.
He rose again all doubts were shed.
How truly had the angel said
  Surrexet Christus Dominus
  Christ has risen from the dead

The Ascension

They saw Him on that Thursday's light,
Ascending from their human sight,
To sit upon the Father's right
  Christus nunc in coelis est,
  Christ is now in Heaven above

Pentecost

A hurricane and shafts of light,
And courage to dispel the night
Of fearfulness. Now all delight in
  Dona Sancti Spiritus.
  Gifts the Holy Spirit gives

The Assumption

She held Him when the Cherubim
Proclaimed His birth with joyful hymn.
But now she reigns supreme with Him,
  Maria nunc assumpta est.
  Assumed is Mary to her Son

The Coronation

O Queen of Heaven, O Queen of earth,
O Queen who gave Our Saviour birth.
Give value to our little worth,
  Maria coronata est
  Mary is crowned in Heaven above

44

THE SORROWS OF MARY

The Sorrows of Mary began when Simeon told Mary in the Temple that a sword of sorrow would pierce her heart. Her final Sorrow was borne as they laid the dead body of Jesus in the tomb. Between these two events christian piety has identified five other Sorrows, and through the years devotion to these sorrowful areas of her life has developed. Some saints have been noted for their devotion to Mary's Sorrows, and loved to dwell on them in hours of contemplation. Saints Bernard and Ambrose have been especially noted for their devotion to the Mother Most Sorrowful. In the thirteenth century the seven founders of the Servite Order devoted themselves in a special way to meditation on Mary's Sorrows, and it is from them that the numeration of seven is said to have come.

The feast of Our Lady of Sorrows was first established at the Provincial Council of Cologne in 1423. The feast received various expressions of ecclesiastical approval, and in 1814 Pope Pius VII established a second feast in honour of the Sorrows of the Mother of God. Today there is a single feast celebrated on 15 September each year.

Dolour beads are not so common as they were earlier in the present century. They consisted of seven small medals, each depicting one of the Sorrows, and these medals were separated by seven beads. They were not unlike the ordinary Rosary beads, except that each 'decade' consisted of seven instead of ten Hail Marys. At the close of the recitation of the Dolour beads the Stabat Mater was often read. However this practice, while appropriate, was essentially a private devotion.

THE SORROWS OF MARY

The Prophecy

He held Him in his arms apart,
He said a sword would ierce her heart,
And prayed that thence he might depart.
    Jam Christum visi Dominum.
    Christ the Lord I've seen at last.

The Exile

They left at once their native land,
To dwell on Egypt's desert sand,
Secure in God's protective hand.
    Familia Sanctissima.
    The Holiest of Families.

The Loss

Within the Temple's vast domain,
For three long days with anxious pain,
She sought Him, longing once again.
    Videre suum Filium.
    To see her most beloved Son

Via Dolorosa

She met Him on that bitter way,
And gazed at Him, upon Him lay,
The Cross that would our ransom pay.
    O Mater Dolorissima.
    O Mother the most sorrowful

Calvary

She stood beside Him as he died,
All soothing help to Him denied,
With heart transfixed, yet dignified.
    Regina stetit omnium.
    There stood the Mother of us all

The Descent	They took Him down when Rome allowed,
	They wrapped Him in a burial shroud,
	While Mary in submission bowed.
	    Dum Corpus tenens Filii.
	    Holding the Body of her Son

The Burial	They placed Him in a borrowed tomb,
	In darkness, silence, sorrow, gloom,
	And death, the fruit of Mary's womb.
	    Sed mox resurget Dominus.
	    But soon the Lord will arise again.

ROSARY MELODY
(for all 4-line verses)

Kevin A. Laheen SJ

Adagio sostenuto